FAVORITE · COOKIE · BARS

FROM CURRENT®

Recipes developed and compiled by the Current Test Kitchens

Photography by Regina Murphy
Food Styling by Lisa Golden Schroeder

©1993 Current, Inc., Colorado Springs, CO 80941
All rights reserved, including the right of reproduction in whole or in part.

ISBN 0-944943-21-7

TABLE·OF·CONTENTS

CHOCOLATE COOKIE BARS

FRUIT COOKIE BARS

OTHER COOKIE BARS

Pictured on cover:
1. Vienna Bars (recipe on page 39)
2. Marbled Brownies (recipe on page 12)
3. Golden Nut Bars (recipe on page 45)

Cutting·Guide

You can change the yield given with each bar cookie recipe by changing the cutting pattern. Generally, the richer the cookie, the smaller the portion. The recommended yield with each cookie recipe is only a guideline.

Yields for 8-inch square or 9-inch square pans or dishes:

16 (about 2") squares

8 (about 4" x 2") bars

12 (about 2½" x 2") bars

32 (about 2" x 1") bars

24 (about 2" x 1¼") bars

Yields for 13 x 9 x 2-inch or 12 x 8 x 2-inch pans or dishes:

24 (about 2") squares

48 (about 1½") squares

36 (about 3" x 1") bars

32 (about 2" x 1½") bars

16 (about 3" x 2") bars

12 (about 4" x 2") bars

30 diamonds* (See Diagram)

Yields for 15½ x 10½ x 1-inch jelly roll pan:

24 (about 2½")squares

70 (about 1½") squares

25 (about 3" x 2") bars

50 (about 3" x 1") bars

75 (about 2" x 1") bars

42 (about 2½" x 1½") bars

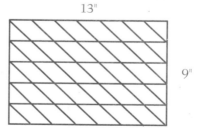

*Cutting Diagram for diamonds

Chocolate • Cookie Bars

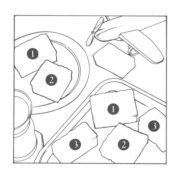

Pictured on page 5:
1. *Orange-Frosted Chocolate Bars (recipe on page 9)*
2. *Chocolate Dream Squares (recipe on page 7)*
3. *Decorated Brownies (recipe on page 16)*

CHOCOLATE·DREAM·SQUARES

Makes 16 (about 2") squares

(Pictured on page 5.)

CHOCOLATE LAYER
- ½ cup butter or margarine
- 2 ounces semisweet chocolate
- 1 cup sugar
- 2 large eggs
- 1 cup all-purpose flour
- ½ cup chopped pecans

FROSTING
- 1½ cups powdered sugar
- 3 tablespoons butter or margarine, softened
- 2 tablespoons milk
- ¾ teaspoon peppermint extract
- Few drops of green food color

GLAZE
- 4 ounces semisweet chocolate
- 2 tablespoons butter or margarine

Preheat oven to 350°. Grease an 8- or 9-inch square baking pan.

To make chocolate layer, melt butter and chocolate in a small saucepan over low heat; cool.

In a small mixer bowl at medium speed, beat sugar, eggs, and chocolate mixture 2 minutes. At low speed, beat in flour and pecans. Spread in pan.

Bake 25 to 30 minutes until center is set. Cool pan on a wire rack.

To make frosting, beat powdered sugar, softened butter, milk, peppermint extract and food color in a small mixer bowl at low speed until smooth. Spread evenly over cooled chocolate layer. Cover and chill 1 hour.

To make glaze, melt chocolate and butter in a small saucepan over low heat; cool. Spread evenly over peppermint layer. Cover and chill 1 hour or until firm. Cut into squares.

Store in an airtight container in a cool, dry place.

S'MORE · SQUARES

Makes 16 (about 2") squares

1 package (11.5 oz.) milk chocolate chips	2 cups miniature marshmallows
2/3 cup light corn syrup	4 cups honey graham cereal
1/4 cup butter or margarine	

Lightly butter an 8- or 9-inch square microwavable baking dish.

In a large microwavable bowl, place chocolate chips, corn syrup, and butter. Cover bowl with plastic wrap.

Microwave at 100% power (700 watts) 2 to 2½ minutes until chocolate is melted and mixture is bubbly. Whisk mixture until blended. Stir in marshmallows. Re-cover and microwave at 100% power 15 seconds. Stir in cereal. Spread in baking dish. Let stand 1 hour or refrigerate just until firm enough to cut into squares.

Store at room temperature.

Orange-Frosted · Chocolate · Bars

Makes 12 (about 2 ½" x 2") bars   (Pictured on page 5.)

Chocolate Layer
- ½ cup butter or margarine
- 2 ounces semisweet chocolate
- ¾ cup sugar
- 2 large eggs
- 1 teaspoon vanilla extract
- ¾ cup all-purpose flour
- ½ teaspoon salt

Frosting
- ¼ cup butter or margarine, softened
- 1 tablespoon frozen orange juice concentrate, thawed
- ½ teaspoon vanilla extract
- 1½ cups powdered sugar, sifted
  Orange food color (optional)

Topping
- 1 ounce semisweet chocolate
- ⅛ teaspoon vegetable oil

Preheat oven to 350°. Grease an 8- or 9-inch square baking pan.

To make chocolate layer, melt butter and chocolate in a small saucepan. Cool.

In a small mixer bowl, beat sugar, eggs, and vanilla. At low speed, beat in chocolate mixture, flour, and salt. Pour into pan.

Bake 25 to 28 minutes until edges and center are set when touched. Cool pan on a wire rack.

To make frosting, beat butter, orange juice concentrate, and vanilla in a small mixer bowl. At low speed, gradually beat in powdered sugar. Tint with orange food color if desired. Spread over chocolate layer. Chill until frosting is firm, about ½ hour.

For topping, melt chocolate with oil. With a small spoon, drizzle thinly over frosting. Chill until topping is firm. Cut into bars.

Mocha·Truffle·Brownies

Makes 24 (about 2" x 1¼") bars

BROWNIE LAYER
- 1¼ cups semisweet chocolate chips (7½ oz.)
- ½ cup butter or margarine
- ¾ cup packed brown sugar
- 2 large eggs
- 1 teaspoon instant coffee powder dissolved in 2 tablespoons water (optional)
- ¾ cup all-purpose flour
- ½ teaspoon baking powder

TRUFFLE FILLING
- 1 cup semisweet chocolate chips (6 oz.)
- 3 teaspoons instant coffee powder
- 1 package (8 oz.) cream cheese, softened
- ⅓ cup powdered sugar

GLAZE
- ¼ cup semisweet chocolate chips (1½ oz.)
- 1 teaspoon solid vegetable shortening

Preheat oven to 350°. Grease an 8- or 9-inch square baking pan.

To make brownie layer, melt 1¼ cups chocolate chips with butter. Cool slightly. In a large mixer bowl at medium speed, beat brown sugar and eggs. Add chocolate mixture and dissolved coffee. Mix well. Stir in flour and baking powder. Spread evenly in pan.

Bake 30 to 35 minutes until a wooden pick inserted in center comes out clean. Cool pan on a wire rack.

To make truffle filling, melt 1 cup chocolate chips with coffee powder. In a small mixer bowl at medium speed, beat cream cheese until smooth. At low speed, beat in chocolate mixture and powdered sugar. Beat until fluffy. Spread over brownies.

To make glaze, melt ¼ cup chocolate chips with shortening. Drizzle over filling. Chill 2 hours. Cut into bars.

Cover and store in the refrigerator.

DOUBLE · CHOCOLATE · BROWNIES

Makes 24 (about 2" x 1¼") bars

1   package (12 oz.) semisweet chocolate
       chips
¼   cup butter or margarine
½   cup sugar
2   tablespoons brown sugar

2   large eggs
½   teaspoon vanilla extract
1   cup all-purpose flour
    Dash of salt
½   cup chopped nuts (optional)

Preheat oven to 325°. Line an 8- or 9-inch square baking pan with foil, extending ends over edges. Grease foil.

In a 1-quart saucepan over low heat, melt ¾ cup of the chocolate chips and butter, stirring until melted. Remove from heat.

Stir in sugar and brown sugar until blended. Stir in eggs, one at a time, beating well after each addition. Stir in vanilla. Stir in flour and salt just until flour is moistened. Stir in remaining 1¼ cups chips. Spread in pan. Sprinkle with nuts, pressing in slightly.

Bake 30 to 35 minutes until top is set and brownie begins to pull away from sides of pan. Cool pan on a wire rack. Holding foil edges, lift brownie from pan. Cut into bars.

Cover tightly with foil and store in a cool place.

MARBLED·BROWNIES

Makes 48 (about 1½") squares   (Pictured on cover.)

2 packages (3 oz. each) cream cheese,
   softened
2⅓ cups sugar
5 large eggs
2 tablespoons all-purpose flour

1¾ teaspoons vanilla extract
4 ounces unsweetened chocolate
½ cup butter or margarine
1¼ cups all-purpose flour
½ teaspoon salt

Preheat oven to 350°. Grease a 13 x 9 x 2-inch baking pan.

In a small mixer bowl at medium speed, beat cream cheese until smooth. Add ⅓ cup of the sugar, 1 of the eggs, 2 tablespoons flour, and ¾ teaspoon of the vanilla and beat until blended. At high speed, beat until smooth; set aside.

In a 3-quart saucepan over low heat, melt chocolate and butter. Remove from heat. Stir in remaining 2 cups sugar. Stir in 4 eggs, one at a time, until blended. Stir in 1¼ cups flour, remaining 1 teaspoon vanilla, and ½ teaspoon salt until smooth. Spread in baking pan. Spoon cream cheese mixture over top and swirl with a spatula to make a marble pattern.

Bake 40 to 45 minutes until a wooden pick inserted in center comes out clean. Cool pan on a wire rack. Cut into squares.

Cover and store in a cool place.

CHOCOLATE·DATE-NUT·BARS

Makes 32 (about 2" x 1½") bars

½ cup butter or margarine
4 ounces unsweetened chocolate
2 cups sugar
4 large eggs
1 cup all-purpose flour

1 cup chopped dates
1 cup chopped nuts
1 teaspoon vanilla extract
½ teaspoon salt

Preheat oven to 350°. Grease a 13 x 9 x 2-inch baking pan.

In a large saucepan over low heat, melt butter and chocolate. Remove from heat. Gradually stir in sugar until well blended. Beat in eggs, one at a time, beating well after each addition. Stir in flour, dates, nuts, vanilla, and salt until smooth. Spread in pan.

Bake 25 to 30 minutes until center is set (do not overbake). Cool pan on a wire rack. Cut into bars.

CALIFORNIA·BROWNIES

Makes 24 (about 2" x 1¼") bars

1   bar (4 oz.) German sweet chocolate
½   cup butter or margarine
3   large eggs
1   cup honey
1½ teaspoons vanilla extract

½   teaspoon almond extract
⅛   teaspoon salt
¾   cup + 1 tablespoon all-purpose flour
½   cup slivered almonds, coarsely chopped

Preheat oven to 350°. Line an 8- or 9-inch square baking pan with foil, extending ends over edges. Grease well.

In a medium saucepan over low heat, melt chocolate and butter.

In a large mixer bowl at high speed, beat eggs, honey, vanilla, almond extract, and salt until well blended. Add chocolate mixture and beat at low speed. Stir in flour and mix well. Spread mixture in pan. Top with almonds.

Bake 40 to 45 minutes until edges just barely pull away from sides of pan. Cool pan on a wire rack. Holding foil edges, lift brownie from pan. Cut into bars.

Easy·Frosted·Brownies

Makes 24 (about 3" x 2½") squares

1 cup sugar	½ cup chopped nuts
¼ cup butter or margarine, softened	1 teaspoon vanilla extract
4 large eggs	½ teaspoon baking powder
1 can (16 oz.) chocolate syrup	1 can (16 oz.) frosting of your choice
1 cup + 1 tablespoon all-purpose flour	

Preheat oven to 350°. Grease a 15½ x 10½ x 1-inch jelly roll pan.

In a large mixer bowl at high speed, beat sugar and butter until creamy. Add eggs and beat until blended. Add syrup, flour, nuts, vanilla, and baking powder and beat at low speed until blended. Spread in baking pan.

Bake 20 to 25 minutes until a wooden pick inserted in center comes out clean. Cool pan on a wire rack. Frost before cutting into squares.

Decorated·Brownies

Makes 42 (about 2½" x 1½") bars (Pictured on page 5.)

2 cups all-purpose flour
2 cups sugar
1 teaspoon baking soda
1 teaspoon ground cinnamon (optional)
1 cup water
½ cup butter or margarine
¼ cup unsweetened cocoa powder

½ cup buttermilk or sour milk
2 large eggs
1 teaspoon vanilla extract
Chocolate Icing (see below)
Corn candy, candy-coated chocolate
  candies, or other small candies

Preheat oven to 400°. Grease a 15½ x 10½ x 1-inch jelly roll pan.

In a large bowl, stir flour, sugar, baking soda, and cinnamon; set aside.

In a small saucepan over medium heat, cook and stir water, butter, and cocoa powder until butter is melted and mixture is smooth; remove from heat and set aside.

In a medium bowl, beat buttermilk, eggs, and vanilla until blended. Stir in chocolate mixture. Pour over dry ingredients and mix until smooth. Spread evenly in jelly roll pan.

Bake 10 to 12 minutes until a wooden pick inserted in center comes out clean. While brownies are baking, make icing. Spread icing on hot brownies. Cool pan on a wire rack.

Decorate with candy. Cut into bars. Store loosely covered in a cool place.

CHOCOLATE ICING: In a 2-quart saucepan over medium heat, cook and stir ½ cup butter or margarine, 5 tablespoons buttermilk or sour milk, and ¼ cup unsweetened cocoa powder until butter is melted and mixture boils. Remove from heat. Gradually stir in 1 pound sifted powdered sugar and 1 teaspoon vanilla extract until smooth. Makes about 2¼ cups.

Brownie·Surprise

Makes 16 (about 2") squares

- 8 maraschino cherries*
- ½ cup butter or margarine, softened
- ⅔ cup sugar
- ⅓ cup honey
- 2 large eggs
- 1½ teaspoons vanilla extract
- ⅔ cup all-purpose flour
- ⅓ cup unsweetened cocoa powder
- ¼ teaspoon salt
- Powdered sugar or frosting of your choice (optional)

Preheat oven to 350°. Grease an 8- or 9-inch square baking pan or coat with non-stick spray.

Cut cherries in half and drain on paper towels; set aside.

In a small mixer bowl at medium speed, beat butter and sugar until fluffy. Beat in honey, eggs, and vanilla until blended. Add flour, cocoa powder, and salt. Beat at low speed about 30 seconds or until smooth and well blended. Pour into pan. Smooth top and arrange cherry halves evenly on top so each serving will have a cherry surprise (cherries will sink during baking).

Bake 33 to 38 minutes until a wooden pick inserted in center comes out clean and top feels firm to the touch. Cool pan on a wire rack. Cut into squares with a sharp knife. Dust tops with powdered sugar or frost.

*If desired, ½ cup small candy-coated chocolate candies can be sprinkled on batter in place of cherry halves.

Microwave·Brownies

Makes 24 (about 2" x 1¼") bars

⅔ cup butter or margarine
½ cup sugar
½ cup packed brown sugar
2 large eggs
1 teaspoon vanilla extract
1 cup all-purpose flour

⅓ cup unsweetened cocoa powder
¼ teaspoon baking powder
⅛ teaspoon salt
¾ cup chopped nuts
Powdered sugar or frosting of your choice

Coat an 8- or 9-inch square microwavable dish or 9-inch microwavable pie plate with non-stick spray.

Place butter in a medium microwavable bowl. Microwave, uncovered, at 100% power (700 watts) 20 to 30 seconds until softened. Stir in sugar and brown sugar until blended. Add eggs and vanilla and beat until well blended. Add flour, cocoa powder, baking powder, and salt and stir just until moistened. Stir in nuts. Spread batter evenly in dish.

Place dish on an inverted small microwavable plate in microwave oven. Microwave, uncovered, at 100% power for 5½ to 7 minutes until a wooden pick inserted in center and in corners comes out clean, rotating dish one-fourth turn every 2 minutes (after 5½ minutes of total cooking, check every 30 seconds).

Cover dish with wax paper and cool on a wire rack 10 minutes. Remove wax paper and cool brownies completely.

To serve, sprinkle with powdered sugar or frost. Cut into bars.

CHOCOLATE · CHERRY · BARS

Makes 25 (about 3" x 2") bars

1   can (21 oz.) cherry pie filling
1   package (18¼ oz.) devil's food cake mix
¼   cup all-purpose flour
1   large egg, beaten

1   tablespoon vegetable oil
1   teaspoon almond extract
1   cup powdered sugar
1   teaspoon milk

Preheat oven to 350°. Grease a 15½ x 10½ x 1-inch jelly roll pan or coat with non-stick spray.

Place 2 tablespoons of the red glaze from the pie filling in a small bowl; set aside for glaze.

In a large bowl with a spoon, mix remaining pie filling, cake mix, flour, egg, oil, and almond extract just until blended. Spread in pan.

Bake 22 to 25 minutes until a wooden pick inserted in center comes out clean. Cool pan on a wire rack 10 minutes.

In a small bowl, mix reserved red glaze, powdered sugar, and milk until well blended. Spread over warm chocolate brownie. Cool completely. Cut into bars.

Store loosely covered.

Cappuccino • Bars

Makes 24 (about 2" x 1¼") bars

1   package (21.5 oz.) fudge brownie mix
¼   cup port wine
2   large eggs
2   tablespoons vegetable oil

2   teaspoons instant coffee powder
1   teaspoon ground cinnamon
½   cup chopped nuts

Preheat oven to 350°. Grease an 8- or 9-inch square baking dish.

In a large bowl, stir brownie mix, port, eggs, oil, coffee powder, and cinnamon until blended (batter will be thick). Stir in nuts. Spread in baking dish.

Bake 25 to 30 minutes until a wooden pick inserted in center comes out clean. Cool dish on a wire rack. Cut into bars.

Caramel · Fudge · Squares

Makes 24 (about 2") squares

1 package (18 oz.) chocolate chocolate chip
    cake mix*
1 cup chopped walnuts

1/3 cup butter or margarine, melted
1/3 cup milk
20 caramel candies, cut in half

Preheat oven to 350°. Grease a 13 x 9 x 2-inch baking pan.

In a medium bowl, mix dry cake mix, nuts, butter, and milk until blended. Spread 2 cups of the dough in pan.

Bake 6 minutes. Sprinkle caramel pieces over baked layer. Make balls with remaining dough, using about 1 1/2 teaspoons for each. Flatten balls and place on top of caramels, covering surface as much as possible. Bake 15 minutes longer (do not overbake). Cool pan on a wire rack at least 15 minutes. Cut into squares.

Once completely cooled, cover and store at room temperature.

*Or use 1 package (21.5 oz.) fudge brownie mix.

CHOCOLATE·PEANUT·O'S

Makes 24 (about 2" x 1¼") bars

3 cups miniature or 28 large
   marshmallows
3 tablespoons water
2 tablespoons honey

1 package (6 oz.) semisweet chocolate chips
   (1 cup)
½ cup peanut butter
3 cups toasted round oat cereal
½ to 1 cup peanuts

Lightly grease an 8- or 9-inch square baking dish.

In a large saucepan, combine marshmallows, water, and honey. Cook over medium heat, stirring constantly with a wooden spoon, until mixture begins to boil. Immediately remove from heat.

Add chips and peanut butter. Stir until chips are melted and mixture is smooth. Immediately stir in cereal and peanuts until cereal is well coated.

Spread mixture evenly in dish and press lightly. Refrigerate 45 minutes or until mixture is firm. Cut into bars.

Store in an airtight container in the refrigerator.

Fruit Cookie Bars

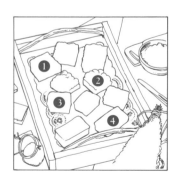

Pictured on page 23:
1. *Cranberry Cheesecake Squares (recipe on page 30)*
2. *Festive Cherry Squares (recipe on page 29)*
3. *Peanut Butter Banana Squares (recipe on page 28)*
4. *Danish Apricot Bars (recipe on page 26)*

APPLE·PIE·SQUARES

Makes 24 (about 2½") squares

3 cups all-purpose flour
1 teaspoon salt
1 cup solid vegetable shortening
7 tablespoons milk
1 large egg yolk
1 cup crushed corn flakes

7 cups peeled, diced tart cooking apples
1 cup sugar
1 teaspoon ground cinnamon
1 large egg white, lightly beaten
   Vanilla Glaze (see below)

Preheat oven to 375°.

Sift flour and salt into a large bowl. With a pastry blender or two knives, cut in shortening until mixture resembles coarse crumbs. In a small bowl, beat milk and egg yolk until blended. Stir into crumb mixture until moistened. Divide into two equal portions. On a lightly floured surface, roll one portion of dough into a 17 x 12-inch rectangle. Transfer to a 15½ x 10½ x 1-inch jelly roll pan, pressing dough up sides of pan. Sprinkle corn flakes in bottom.

In a large bowl, stir apples, sugar, and cinnamon until well mixed. Spread evenly over corn flakes. Roll remaining dough into a rectangle, 1 inch larger than pan, and place on top of apples, lightly pressing edges to seal. Pierce top with a fork to permit steam to escape during baking. Brush top with egg white.

Bake 50 to 60 minutes until golden brown. Spread top with glaze while still warm. Cut into squares. Serve warm or at room temperature.

VANILLA GLAZE: In a small bowl, stir 1 cup powdered sugar, 2 tablespoons water, and 1 teaspoon vanilla extract until smooth. Makes about ½ cup.

Danish·Apricot·Bars

Makes 32 (about 2" x 1½") bars   (Pictured on page 23.)

1	package active dry yeast
¼	cup warm water (105° to 115°)
2¼	cups all-purpose flour
¾	cup sugar
½	teaspoon salt
1	cup butter or margarine

1	large egg, slightly beaten
1	jar (10 oz.) apricot preserves
1	cup coarsely chopped pecans
4	ounces dried apricots, finely chopped
	Powdered sugar

In a small bowl, dissolve yeast in warm water; let stand until foamy, 5 to 10 minutes.

In a medium bowl, mix flour, ½ cup of the sugar, and salt. With a pastry blender or two knives, cut in butter until pieces are the size of small peas. Add egg and yeast mixture; blend until mixture forms a ball. Divide dough into two equal portions. Cover and chill at least 30 minutes or up to 2 hours.

In a medium bowl, combine preserves, pecans, dried apricots, and remaining ¼ cup sugar; set aside.

Preheat oven to 375°. Grease a 13 x 9 x 2-inch baking pan.

On a lightly floured surface, roll one portion of dough into a 13 x 9-inch rectangle. Carefully fit into pan. Evenly spread apricot filling over dough to within ½ inch of all edges. Roll remaining dough into a 13 x 9-inch rectangle. Place on top of fruit mixture; lightly press edges to seal.

Bake 25 to 30 minutes until golden brown. Cool pan on a wire rack.

Store tightly covered in a cool place up to 3 days. Cut into bars. Just before serving, dust with powdered sugar.

Apricot-Pineapple·Squares

Makes 48 (about 1½") squares

1½	cups all-purpose flour	1	cup sugar
1	teaspoon baking powder	¼	cup butter or margarine, melted
½	cup butter or margarine	1	large egg
1	large egg, beaten	1	teaspoon vanilla extract
3	to 4 tablespoons milk	1½	cups chopped pecans
1⅓	cups apricot-pineapple preserves	1	cup flaked coconut

Preheat oven to 350°. Grease a 13 x 9 x 2-inch baking pan or coat with non-stick spray.

In a medium bowl, mix flour and baking powder. With a pastry blender or two knives, cut in ½ cup butter until mixture resembles coarse crumbs. Stir in beaten egg and milk until flour mixture is moistened. Press dough into baking pan. Evenly spread preserves over dough to within ¼ inch of all edges.

In a medium bowl, stir sugar, melted butter, egg, and vanilla until well blended. Stir in nuts and coconut. Spread over preserves in pan.

Bake 35 to 45 minutes until top is browned. Cool pan on a wire rack.

Chill before cutting into squares.

Peanut·Butter·Banana·Squares

Makes 16 (about 2") squares   (Pictured on page 23.)

1 cup plus 2 tablespoons all-purpose flour	2 large eggs
½ teaspoon baking soda	1 small ripe banana, mashed
¼ teaspoon salt	1 teaspoon vanilla extract
½ cup peanut butter	1 cup walnut pieces
⅓ cup butter or margarine, softened	1 package (6 oz.) semisweet chocolate chips
½ cup packed brown sugar	(1 cup)
½ cup sugar	Powdered sugar (optional)

Preheat oven to 350°. Butter an 8- or 9-inch square baking pan.

In a small bowl, mix flour, baking soda, and salt; set aside.

In a large mixer bowl at medium speed, beat peanut butter and butter until well blended. Gradually beat in brown sugar and sugar until light and fluffy. Add eggs, one at a time, and beat well after each addition. Beat in banana and vanilla. Add dry ingredients and beat just until blended. Stir in nuts and chips. Spread in baking pan.

Bake 35 to 40 minutes until cake pulls away from pan. Cool pan on a wire rack. Cut into squares.

Cover with plastic wrap. Serve the next day. Sprinkle with powdered sugar if desired.

FESTIVE · CHERRY · SQUARES

Makes 24 (about 2") squares   (Pictured on page 23.)

CRUST
  2 cups graham cracker crumbs
  1/3 cup butter or margarine, melted

FILLING
  2 packages (3 oz. each) cream cheese,
      softened
  1 cup sugar

  3 large eggs
  2 cups flaked coconut
  1/2 cup plain yogurt or dairy sour cream
  3 tablespoons all-purpose flour

TOPPING
  1 can (21 oz.) cherry pie filling

Preheat oven to 350°. Grease a 13 x 9 x 2-inch baking pan or coat with non-stick spray.

To make crust, mix graham cracker crumbs and melted butter. Press evenly in bottom of pan.

Bake 10 minutes. (Leave oven on.) Cool on a wire rack.

To make filling, beat cream cheese in a medium mixer bowl with electric mixer until smooth. Gradually beat in sugar. Beat in eggs. Add coconut, yogurt, and flour. On low speed, beat until well blended. Carefully spread evenly over crust to within 1/4 inch of edges.

Bake 30 minutes or until set. Cool pan on a wire rack 10 minutes. Spoon pie filling evenly over filling.

Chill at least 1 hour. Cut into squares with a sharp knife. Store loosely covered in the refrigerator.

CRANBERRY·CHEESECAKE·SQUARES

Makes 16 (about 2") squares

(Pictured on page 23.)

1 cup all-purpose flour	1 large egg
1/4 cup sugar	1 teaspoon vanilla extract
1/2 cup butter or margarine	1 can (16 oz.) jellied cranberry sauce
1 package (8 oz.) cream cheese, softened	1/3 cup finely chopped walnuts
1/3 cup sugar	

Preheat oven to 350°. Grease an 8- or 9-inch square baking pan.

In a small bowl, mix flour and 1/4 cup sugar. With a pastry blender or two knives, cut in butter until mixture resembles coarse crumbs. Press crumbs into bottom of baking pan.

Bake 20 minutes or until golden brown. Cool pan on a wire rack.

In a small mixer bowl at medium speed, beat cream cheese, 1/3 cup sugar, egg, and vanilla until smooth.

With a fork, break up cranberry sauce. Spread over cooled crust. Top with cream cheese mixture. Sprinkle top with walnuts.

Bake 35 minutes. Cool pan on wire rack.

Store in the refrigerator. Cut into squares and serve cold.

CITRUS·DATE·BARS

Makes 36 (about 3" x 1") bars

1¼ cups all-purpose flour
½ teaspoon baking powder
¼ teaspoon salt
¾ cup butter or margarine
¾ cup sugar

1 large egg
2 teaspoons grated orange rind
1 package (8 oz.) chopped dates
1 cup coarsely chopped pecans
  Orange Cream Cheese Icing (see below)

Preheat oven to 325°. Coat a 13 x 9 x 2-inch baking pan with non-stick spray.

In a small bowl, stir together flour, baking powder, and salt; set aside.

Melt butter in a large saucepan over low heat. Remove from heat. Stir in flour mixture, sugar, egg, orange rind, dates, and pecans, mixing well. Spread batter in pan.

Bake 25 to 30 minutes until lightly browned and edges begin to pull away from sides of pan. Cool pan on a wire rack.

Frost with Orange Cream Cheese Icing. Cut into bars with a sharp knife.

Cover and store in the refrigerator.

ORANGE CREAM CHEESE ICING: In a small bowl, stir 1 package (3 oz.) softened cream cheese, 1 cup sifted powdered sugar, and 1 teaspoon grated orange rind until well blended.

TENDER·LEMON·SQUARES

Makes 16 (about 2") squares

1 cup all-purpose flour	2 tablespoons all-purpose flour
1/2 cup butter or margarine, softened	1 tablespoon grated lemon rind
1 1/4 cups powdered sugar	3 tablespoons lemon juice
1 tablespoon water	1/2 teaspoon baking powder
1 cup sugar	1/4 teaspoon salt
2 large eggs	1 tablespoon butter or margarine, softened

Preheat oven to 350°.

In a large mixer bowl at low speed, beat 1 cup flour, 1/2 cup butter, 1/4 cup of the powdered sugar, and water until blended. Press firmly into bottom and 1/2 inch up sides of an 8- or 9-inch square baking dish.

Bake 15 to 20 minutes until edges are lightly browned.

In a small mixer bowl at high speed, beat sugar, eggs, 2 tablespoons flour, lemon rind, 2 tablespoons of the lemon juice, baking powder, and salt until light and fluffy. Pour evenly over hot crust.

Bake 25 to 30 minutes longer until center is set. Cool dish on a wire rack.

In a small mixer bowl at low speed, beat remaining 1 cup powdered sugar, 1 tablespoon butter, and remaining 1 tablespoon lemon juice until smooth and of spreading consistency. Spread over top of baked mixture. Cut into squares.

Store loosely covered.

LIME·CHEESECAKE·SQUARES

Makes 16 (about 2") squares

2   large limes
1   cup graham cracker crumbs
¼   cup butter or margarine, melted
1   tablespoon sugar
2   packages (8 oz. each) cream cheese,
      softened

⅔   cup sugar
2   large eggs
⅔   cup dairy sour cream
1   tablespoon cornstarch
⅛   teaspoon salt

Preheat oven to 325°. Line an 8- or 9-inch square baking pan with foil, extending ends over edges.

Grate 1 tablespoon of peel from lime. Squeeze 2 tablespoons juice and set both aside.

In a small bowl, stir graham cracker crumbs, butter, and 1 tablespoon sugar until blended. Press evenly into bottom of pan.

In a medium mixer bowl, beat cream cheese until smooth. Add ⅔ cup sugar and eggs and beat well. At low speed, beat in ⅓ cup of the sour cream, lime juice and rind, cornstarch, and salt until blended. Pour over crust.

Bake 40 to 45 minutes until set. Cool pan on a wire rack 10 minutes. Carefully spread remaining ⅓ cup sour cream over top. Cool pan on a wire rack until room temperature.

Chill at least 1 hour. Holding foil edges, lift cookie from pan. Cut into squares and serve cold. Cover and store in the refrigerator.

Mincemeat•Diamonds

Makes about 30 (about 1¼") diamonds

2 large eggs	1¼ cups all-purpose flour
1 cup prepared mincemeat	¼ teaspoon baking soda
½ cup packed brown sugar	1 cup chopped walnuts
2 tablespoons vegetable oil	Cream Cheese Frosting (see below)
1 teaspoon brandy or vanilla extract (optional)	

Preheat oven to 350°. Generously grease a 13 x 9 x 2-inch baking pan or coat with non-stick spray.

In a large bowl, whisk eggs until well beaten. Stir in mincemeat, brown sugar, oil, and extract. Stir in flour and baking soda until well blended. Stir in nuts. Spread batter in pan.

Bake 25 minutes or until wooden pick inserted in center comes out clean. Cool pan on a wire rack.

Frost. If desired, lightly score top with a fork to create a decorative pattern. Chill. Cut into diamonds (see page 4) or bars with a sharp knife. Cover and store in the refrigerator.

CREAM CHEESE FROSTING: In a small mixer bowl at medium speed, beat 1 package (3 oz.) softened cream cheese until smooth. At low speed, gradually beat in 2 cups powdered sugar and ½ teaspoon brandy or vanilla extract until of spreading consistency.

ORANGE-PECAN·BARS

Makes 32 (about 2" x 1½") bars

1	cup butter or margarine, softened	2½	cups all-purpose flour
1	cup sugar	1½	cups finely chopped pecans
1	large egg	1¼	cups orange marmalade
	Pinch of salt		Sugar

Preheat oven to 375°. Grease and flour a 13 x 9 x 2-inch baking pan.

In a large mixer bowl at medium speed, beat butter until light and fluffy. Gradually beat in 1 cup sugar, egg, and salt. At low speed, gradually beat in flour and nuts until moistened and well blended. Reserve 1½ cups of the mixture for topping. Pat remaining mixture into pan and press lightly. Evenly spread marmalade over dough to within ½ inch of all edges. Sprinkle reserved crumb mixture over marmalade. Sprinkle surface with sugar.

Bake 30 to 40 minutes until medium brown. Cool pan on a wire rack. While warm, cut into bars.

Cover and store in a cool place.

CRUMB-TOPPED·PRUNE·BARS

Makes 24 (about 2" x 1¼") bars

PRUNE FILLING
- ¾ cup chopped pitted prunes
- ⅓ cup orange juice
- ¼ cup sugar
- 1 teaspoon vanilla extract
- 1 cup chopped walnuts

CRUST
- 2 tablespoons dairy sour cream
- 1 teaspoon vanilla extract
- 1½ cups all-purpose flour
- ½ cup butter or margarine, softened
- ⅓ cup sugar
- ½ teaspoon baking powder
- ⅛ teaspoon salt

Preheat oven to 375°.

To make filling, cook and stir prunes and orange juice in a small saucepan over medium heat until mixture boils. Reduce heat to low, cover, and simmer 5 minutes or until prunes are very soft. Stir in ¼ cup sugar. Remove from heat.

Stir in 1 teaspoon vanilla, then walnuts. Cool to room temperature.

To make crust, stir sour cream and 1 teaspoon vanilla in a large mixer bowl until blended. Add flour, butter, ⅓ cup sugar, baking powder, and salt. At low speed, beat until butter is in fine pieces and mixture is crumbly. Set 1 cup of the mixture aside.

Press remaining crumb mixture in an ungreased 8- or 9-inch square baking pan. Carefully spread filling over crust. Sprinkle reserved crumb mixture over the top, pressing down lightly.

Bake 25 to 30 minutes until top is golden brown. Cool pan on a wire rack.

Chill 30 minutes, then cut into bars with a sharp knife. Store in a loosely covered container in a cool place.

OLD-FASHIONED · RAISIN · OAT · BARS

Makes 32 (about 2" x 1½") bars

2	large eggs	1	teaspoon baking soda
3	teaspoons vanilla extract	¾	teaspoon ground cinnamon
1½	cups raisins	¾	teaspoon salt
⅔	cup butter or margarine, softened	1⅓	cups quick or old-fashioned oats
⅔	cup packed brown sugar	¾	cup chopped nuts (optional)
½	cup sugar		Powdered sugar (optional)
1¾	cups all-purpose flour		

Preheat oven to 350°. Lightly grease a 13 x 9 x 2-inch baking pan or coat with non-stick spray.

In a medium bowl, whisk together eggs and vanilla. Stir in raisins. Let stand 30 minutes, stirring occasionally.

Meanwhile, in a large mixer bowl at medium speed, beat butter, brown sugar, and sugar. Add flour, baking soda, cinnamon, and salt and beat at low speed until blended. Stir in raisin mixture, oats, and nuts. (Mixture will be stiff.) Press evenly in pan.

Bake 28 to 30 minutes until light brown and top springs back when lightly touched. Do not overbake. Cool pan on a wire rack. Cut into bars with a sharp knife.

Store in a covered container. If desired, roll in powdered sugar just before serving.

Raisin·Spice·Squares

Makes 48 (about 2½") squares

1½	cups sugar	2	cups all-purpose flour
1	cup butter or margarine, softened	1	teaspoon ground nutmeg
3	large eggs	1	teaspoon ground cinnamon
¼	cup milk	1½	cups raisins
½	teaspoon baking soda	½	cup chopped walnuts or pecans
	Pinch of salt		

Preheat oven to 375°. Generously grease two 15½ x 10½ x 1-inch jelly roll pans.

In a large mixer bowl at medium speed, beat sugar and butter until creamy; beat in eggs. Mix together milk, baking soda, and salt; at low speed beat into creamed mixture. Beat in flour, nutmeg, and cinnamon until well blended. Stir in raisins and nuts. Spread in pans.

Bake 10 to 12 minutes. Cut into squares while still hot. Cool pans on wire racks.

NOTE: If baking both jelly roll pans at the same time, switch oven position after 5 minutes.

Vienna • Bars

Makes 32 (about 2" x 1") bars   (Pictured on cover.)

2 cups all-purpose flour
1¼ cups ground blanched almonds
½ cup sugar
1½ teaspoons grated lemon rind
1 teaspoon ground cinnamon

⅛ teaspoon salt
½ cup butter or margarine
2 large eggs, beaten
½ cup red raspberry or strawberry preserves
¼ cup red currant jelly

Preheat oven to 350°.

In a large bowl, mix flour, almonds, sugar, lemon rind, cinnamon, and salt. With a pastry blender or two knives, cut in butter until mixture resembles coarse crumbs. Add eggs and toss with a fork until mixture is evenly moistened and holds together. Press 1½ cups of the mixture into the bottom and ¼ inch up sides of an 8- or 9-inch square baking dish.

Spread preserves evenly over pastry in dish. On a lightly floured surface, roll remaining pastry mixture to ¼-inch thickness. Cut into ½-inch strips. Arrange a lattice of diagonal strips over top. Press strips and bottom layer of pastry together at edges.

Bake 40 minutes or until pastry is lightly browned. Place dish on a wire rack.

In a small saucepan over low heat, stir jelly until melted and smooth. With a pastry brush, spread jelly over top of baked mixture. Cool before cutting into bars.

Store loosely covered in a cool place.

Christmas•Bars

Makes 50 (about 3" x 1") bars

1³⁄₄   cups all-purpose flour
1¹⁄₂   teaspoons ground cinnamon
¹⁄₂   teaspoon baking soda
¹⁄₄   teaspoon ground cloves
¹⁄₄   teaspoon ground nutmeg
¹⁄₄   teaspoon salt
²⁄₃   cup vegetable oil
¹⁄₂   cup packed brown sugar

¹⁄₄   cup sugar
¹⁄₄   cup honey
1   large egg
1   teaspoon vanilla extract
1¹⁄₂   cups mixed candied fruit, chopped
1   cup chopped walnuts or pecans
    Lemon Drizzle (see page 57)

Preheat oven to 375°. Grease a 15¹⁄₂ x 10¹⁄₂ x 1-inch jelly roll pan.

In a medium bowl, stir flour, cinnamon, baking soda, cloves, nutmeg, and salt; set aside.

In a large bowl, stir oil, brown sugar, sugar, honey, egg, and vanilla until well blended. Stir in flour mixture until moistened. Stir in fruit and nuts until well mixed. With lightly floured fingers, pat dough evenly in pan.

Bake 15 minutes or until golden brown and a wooden pick inserted in center comes out clean. Cool slightly on a wire rack. While still warm, cut into bars with a sharp knife. When cool, glaze with Lemon Drizzle.

Store loosely covered. If making ahead, store without drizzle. Cover tightly with foil up to 2 days. One to two hours before serving, glaze with drizzle.

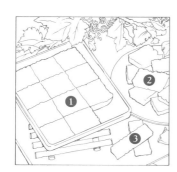

Pictured on page 41:
1. Candy Bar Cookies (recipe on page 46)
2. Caramel Oat Delights (recipe on page 58)
3. Gingered Shortbread (recipe on page 57)

EUROPEAN·ALMOND·COOKIES

Makes 24 (about 2") squares or 48 triangles

½	cup all-purpose flour	1	can (8 oz.) almond paste
½	teaspoon baking powder	⅔	cup sliced almonds
⅔	cup sugar	3	tablespoons sugar
2	large eggs		

Preheat oven to 350°. Line a 13 x 9 x 2-inch baking pan with foil, extending foil over edge of pan. Coat with non-stick spray.

In a small bowl, stir flour and baking powder; set aside.

In a medium mixer bowl at medium speed, beat ⅔ cup sugar and eggs until thick and lemon colored. Gradually add almond paste and beat until well blended. By hand, fold in flour mixture. Spread in pan. Sprinkle almonds and 3 tablespoons sugar over top.

Bake 30 minutes or until edges are light brown and top is set. Do not overbake. Cool pan on a wire rack. Holding foil edges, lift cookie from pan. Cut into squares. If desired, cut each square diagonally to form triangles.

Cover and store in a cool place.

MACADAMIA·NUT·BARS

Makes about 54 (1½" x 1") bars

1   cup all-purpose flour
1   jar (3½ oz.) macadamia nuts, coarsely
     chopped
¼ teaspoon baking powder
¼ teaspoon salt

½ cup butter or margarine, softened
½ cup packed brown sugar
1 large egg yolk
1 teaspoon vanilla extract
1 large egg white, lightly beaten

Preheat oven to 325°. Generously grease a baking sheet.

In a medium bowl, stir flour, ¼ cup of the nuts, baking powder, and salt; set aside.

In a large mixer bowl at medium speed, beat butter, brown sugar, egg yolk, and vanilla until well blended, scraping bowl occasionally. At low speed, beat in flour mixture until well mixed, scraping bowl as needed.

Spoon dough onto center of baking sheet. Cover with wax paper and, with a rolling pin, roll into a rectangle ¼ inch thick. Remove wax paper. Brush surface of dough with egg white and sprinkle with remaining nuts.

Bake 22 to 25 minutes until golden brown. Remove from oven and, with a sharp knife, immediately cut into bars. Cool bars on baking sheet 5 minutes. Transfer cookies to wire racks to cool completely.

Cover and store in a cool place.

Golden · Nut · Bars

Makes 32 (about 2" x 1½") bars or 64 triangles   (Pictured on cover.)

1½ cups all-purpose flour
 ¾ cup packed brown sugar
 ½ cup butter, softened
 ¼ teaspoon salt

 ¾ cup butterscotch chips
 ½ cup light corn syrup
 2 tablespoons butter
 1 can (12 oz.) salted mixed nuts

Preheat oven to 350°.

In a medium bowl, mix flour, brown sugar, ½ cup butter, and salt with a fork until mixture resembles coarse crumbs. Pat into an ungreased 13 x 9 x 2-inch baking pan.

Bake 10 minutes. Remove from oven.

Meanwhile, in a small saucepan over low heat, melt butterscotch chips, corn syrup, and 2 tablespoons butter, stirring until smooth. Remove from heat.

Spread mixed nuts over baked crust. Drizzle butterscotch mixture over top, covering completely.

Bake 10 minutes or until edges are bubbly. Loosen edges from sides of pan with a knife. Cool pan on a wire rack. Cut into bars or triangles with a sharp knife.

Cover and store. May be frozen up to 2 months.

Candy·Bar·Cookies

Makes 12 (about 2½" x 2") bars

(Pictured on page 41.)

½ cup butter or margarine	½ teaspoon vanilla extract
½ cup packed brown sugar	¾ cup butterscotch chips
1 cup quick-cooking oats	⅔ cup light corn syrup
½ cup all-purpose flour	1 tablespoon vegetable oil
½ teaspoon baking powder	1½ cups roasted salted peanuts

Place butter in a 1-quart microwavable bowl. Microwave, uncovered, at 100% power (700 watts) 20 to 30 seconds until softened. With a wooden spoon, beat in brown sugar until creamy. Stir in oats, flour, baking powder, and vanilla until blended. With floured fingers, press evenly in bottom of an ungreased 8- or 9-inch square microwavable dish.

Microwave, uncovered, at 100% power 3 to 4 minutes until puffed and bubbly, rotating dish one-half turn after 2 minutes. Set aside on a wire rack.

In a 4-cup microwavable measuring cup or bowl, combine butterscotch chips, corn syrup, and oil. Microwave, uncovered, at 100% power 3 to 4 minutes until chips are melted and mixture is blended, whisking every minute.

Sprinkle nuts on cookie base. Evenly pour butterscotch mixture over nuts to coat. Cool completely. Cut into bars with a sharp knife.

Cover and store in the refrigerator. Let stand at room temperature 10 minutes before serving.

TEMPTATION·BARS

Makes 32 (about 2" x 1½") bars

- ½ cup butter or margarine
- 1 cup graham cracker crumbs
- 1 cup shredded coconut
- 1 package (6 oz.) semisweet chocolate chips (1 cup)

- 1 cup peanut butter chips
- 1 can (14 oz.) sweetened condensed milk
- 1 cup coarsely chopped unsalted dry roasted peanuts

Preheat oven to 350°.

Melt butter in a 13 x 9 x 2-inch baking pan (do not brown). Spread over bottom of pan. Evenly layer graham cracker crumbs, then coconut, chocolate chips, and peanut butter chips. Evenly pour condensed milk over chips. Sprinkle with peanuts.

Bake 25 to 30 minutes until lightly browned around edges. Cool pan on a wire rack until room temperature. Chill until set. Cut into bars.

Cover and store in a cool, dry place.

Layered · Coconut · Bars

Makes 24 (about 2" x 1¼") bars

½ cup butter or margarine	1 cup milk chocolate chips
1 cup graham cracker crumbs	1 cup coarsely chopped nuts
1 cup flaked coconut	1 can (14 oz.) sweetened condensed milk

P reheat oven to 350°.

Melt butter in an 8- or 9-inch square baking pan. Evenly layer graham cracker crumbs, then coconut, chips, and nuts. Evenly pour condensed milk over nuts.

Bake 30 to 35 minutes until golden brown on top. Cool pan on a wire rack. Cut into bars.

Cover and store in a cool place.

CRUNCHY·BUTTERSCOTCH·SQUARES

Makes 16 (about 2") squares

1/3 cup butter or margarine	1 cup butterscotch chips
4 1/2 cups corn flakes, crushed	1 cup coarsely chopped nuts
1 cup flaked coconut	1 can (14 oz.) sweetened condensed milk

Preheat oven to 350°.

Melt butter in an 8-inch square baking dish. Evenly layer corn flake crumbs, then coconut, butterscotch chips, and nuts. Evenly pour condensed milk over nuts.

Bake 30 to 35 minutes until golden brown on top. Cool dish on a wire rack. Cut into squares.

Cover and store in a cool place.

Pecan·Bars

Makes 32 (about 2" x 1½") bars

2⅓ cups all-purpose flour	½ cup packed brown sugar
⅔ cup sugar	2 teaspoons vanilla extract
½ cup butter or margarine	1 teaspoon salt
1½ cups dark corn syrup	1 cup chopped pecans
4 large eggs	

Preheat oven to 350°. Grease a 13 x 9 x 2-inch baking dish.

In a medium bowl, mix 2 cups of the flour and sugar. With a pastry blender or two knives, cut in butter until mixture resembles coarse crumbs. Press mixture evenly against bottom and ½ inch up sides of dish.

Bake 25 minutes or until lightly browned.

Meanwhile, in a small mixer bowl at high speed, beat corn syrup, eggs, brown sugar, remaining ⅓ cup flour, vanilla, and salt until smooth. Pour over baked crust. Sprinkle with pecans. Reduce oven temperature to 325°.

Bake 60 minutes or until center is set. Cool dish on a wire rack. Cut into bars.

Cover and store in a cool place.

CARROT-PECAN·SQUARES

Makes 48 (about 1 ½") squares

2	cups all-purpose flour	½	cup butter or margarine, softened
¾	teaspoon ground cinnamon	2	large eggs
¾	teaspoon ground nutmeg	1¼	cups finely shredded carrots
½	teaspoon ground cloves	1	cup golden raisins
¼	teaspoon baking soda	1	cup coarsely chopped nuts
¼	teaspoon salt	48	pecan halves
1	cup packed brown sugar		

Preheat oven to 350°. Grease and flour a 13 x 9 x 2-inch baking pan or coat with non-stick spray.

In a medium bowl, stir flour, cinnamon, nutmeg, cloves, baking soda, and salt; set aside.

In a large mixer bowl at medium speed, beat brown sugar and butter until fluffy. Beat in eggs. At low speed, beat in carrots, raisins, and chopped nuts until blended. Beat in flour mixture until all ingredients are moistened. Spread in pan. Arrange pecan halves in rows (8 halves along long side and 6 halves across).

Bake 28 to 30 minutes until a wooden pick inserted in center comes out clean. Cool pan on a wire rack.

Cover and store overnight. Cut into squares with a sharp knife.

Praline-Pumpkin · Bars

Makes 32 (about 2" x 1½") bars

¼ cup butter or margarine	1 teaspoon vanilla extract
¾ cup all-purpose flour	½ teaspoon baking powder
¾ cup packed brown sugar	½ teaspoon baking soda
¾ cup canned pumpkin	½ teaspoon salt
2 large eggs	Praline Topping (see below)
2 teaspoons pumpkin pie spice	

Preheat oven to 350°. Grease a 13 x 9 x 2-inch baking pan.

In a medium saucepan over low heat, melt butter. Remove from heat. Beat in flour, brown sugar, pumpkin, eggs, pumpkin pie spice, vanilla, baking powder, baking soda, and salt until smooth. Spread batter in prepared pan. Sprinkle Praline Topping evenly over top.

Bake 20 to 25 minutes until a wooden pick inserted in center comes out clean. Cool pan on a wire rack. Cut into bars.

Praline Topping: In a small saucepan, melt ¼ cup butter or margarine. Add 1 cup coarsely chopped pecans and ¾ cup packed brown sugar. Cook and stir over medium heat until bubbly. Remove from heat and set aside. Makes about 1½ cups.

PISTACHIO·BARS

Makes 32 (about 2" x 1½") bars

1½	cups butter or margarine, softened	1	cup chopped pistachio nuts
¾	cup sugar	1	tablespoon sugar
3	cups all-purpose flour		

P reheat oven to 325°.

In a medium mixer bowl at medium speed, beat butter and ¾ cup sugar until fluffy. At low speed, gradually beat in flour. Press evenly in bottom of an ungreased 13 x 9 x 2-inch baking pan. Sprinkle with pistachio nuts. Press lightly into dough. Sprinkle with 1 tablespoon sugar.

Bake 50 to 60 minutes until golden. Cut into bars while still hot. Cool pan on a wire rack.

Meringue·Squares

Makes 16 (about 2") squares

³⁄₄ cup all-purpose flour	¹⁄₂ teaspoon vanilla extract
¹⁄₂ teaspoon salt	2 large egg whites
¹⁄₂ teaspoon ground nutmeg	¹⁄₈ teaspoon cream of tartar
¹⁄₂ cup packed brown sugar	¹⁄₂ cup sugar
¹⁄₄ cup butter or margarine	1 cup chopped walnuts
2 large egg yolks	

Preheat oven to 350°. Grease an 8- or 9-inch square baking dish.

In a small bowl, stir together flour, salt, and nutmeg; set aside.

In a small saucepan, combine brown sugar and butter. Over medium heat, cook until mixture begins to bubble. Remove from heat and let cool.

Beat in egg yolks and vanilla. Stir in flour mixture. Spread in baking dish.

In a small mixer bowl, beat egg whites and cream of tartar until soft peaks form; gradually beat in sugar, 1 tablespoon at a time. Beat until very stiff peaks form and whites are glossy. Fold in nuts; spread over dough.

Bake 30 minutes or until lightly browned. Cool dish on a wire rack. Cut into squares.

MAPLE·WALNUT·SQUARES

Makes 70 (about 1½") squares

2	cups all-purpose flour		2	large egg yolks
½	teaspoon salt		1	tablespoon water
1	cup solid vegetable shortening		3	teaspoons liquid maple flavor
½	cup sugar		2	large egg whites
1½	cups packed brown sugar		¾	cup finely chopped walnuts

Preheat oven to 375°. Grease a 15½ x 10½ x 1-inch jelly roll pan.

In a small bowl, mix flour and salt; set aside.

In a large mixer bowl at medium speed, beat shortening until creamy. Gradually beat in sugar and ½ cup of the brown sugar. Add egg yolks and continue beating until light and fluffy. Beat in water and 2 teaspoons of the maple flavor. Add flour mixture and beat until well blended. Spread batter evenly in pan.

In a small mixer bowl at high speed, beat egg whites until soft peaks form. Reduce speed to low and gradually beat in remaining 1 cup brown sugar and remaining 1 teaspoon maple flavor. Increase speed to high and beat until fluffy. With a metal spatula, spread egg white mixture over batter; sprinkle with walnuts and pat lightly into meringue.

Bake 20 minutes or until meringue is set and dry on top. Cool pan on a wire rack at least 2 hours. Cut into squares.

Best served same day. Lightly cover leftovers and store in a cool place.

HUNGARIAN·POPPY·SEED·BARS

Makes 24 (about 2" x 1¼") bars

¾ cup butter or margarine, softened
¾ cup packed brown sugar
1 teaspoon vanilla extract
¾ cup all-purpose flour

1 teaspoon baking soda
2¼ cups quick-cooking oats
1 can (12½ oz.) prepared poppy seed
    filling

Preheat oven to 350°. Line an 8- or 9-inch square baking pan with foil, extending ends over edges. Grease foil.

In a large mixer bowl at medium speed, beat butter and brown sugar until fluffy. Beat in vanilla. At low speed, beat in flour and baking soda. Beat in 2 cups of the oats until combined. Set ½ cup of the mixture aside. Pat remaining mixture into pan, flouring fingers if needed. Spread filling over. Add remaining ¼ cup oats to reserved topping. Crumble topping mixture over poppy seed filling and pat gently.

Bake 30 minutes or until lightly browned. Cool pan on a wire rack, loosening from edge of pan while warm. Holding foil edges, lift cookie from pan. Cut into bars.

Store loosely covered.

HIGH ALTITUDE ADJUSTMENT: At 6,000 feet, decrease baking soda to ½ teaspoon.

GINGERED·SHORTBREAD

Makes 28 (3" x 1") bars

(Pictured on page 41.)

2 cups all-purpose flour
1 cup butter, softened
¹⁄₂ cup powdered sugar

1 teaspoon ground ginger
Lemon Drizzle (see below)

Preheat oven to 350°.

In a medium bowl, mix flour, butter, powdered sugar, and ginger with a fork until well blended and forms a dough. On an ungreased baking sheet, pat dough into a 14 x 6-inch rectangle. Score dough deeply with the tines of a fork or a knife, dividing rectangle in half lengthwise and cutting 1-inch bars crosswise. Crimp edges if desired.

Bake 20 to 25 minutes until set and light golden brown. Cool completely on baking sheet on a wire rack. Glaze with Lemon Drizzle and break into bars along scored lines.

LEMON DRIZZLE: In a small bowl, combine 1 cup sifted powdered sugar, 2 teaspoons corn syrup, and 1 teaspoon grated lemon rind. Stir in 4¹⁄₂ to 5¹⁄₂ teaspoons lemon juice until desired consistency. Tint with 1 to 2 drops yellow food color if desired. Use on Gingered Shortbread or on cookies of your choice. Makes about ²⁄₃ cup.

Caramel · Oat · Delights

Makes 32 (2" x 1½") bars

(Pictured on page 41.)

32	light caramels	¼	teaspoon salt
5	tablespoons half-and-half	1	cup quick-cooking oats
¾	cup butter or margarine, melted	1	package (6 oz.) semisweet chocolate
¾	cup packed brown sugar		chips (1 cup)
1	cup all-purpose flour	1	cup chopped pecans
½	teaspoon baking soda		

Preheat oven to 350°. Grease a 13 x 9 x 2-inch baking pan.

In a medium saucepan over low heat, melt caramels in half-and-half. Stir until smooth; set aside.

In a medium bowl, mix butter and brown sugar. Stir in flour, baking soda, and salt. Stir in oats. Set 1¼ cups of the mixture aside. Press remaining mixture into bottom of pan. Sprinkle with chocolate chips and nuts. Drizzle with caramel mixture. Sprinkle remaining crumb mixture on top.

Bake 15 to 20 minutes until golden brown. Cool baking dish on a wire rack. Chill at least 1 hour before cutting into bars.

Vanilla·Squares

Makes 16 (about 2") squares

1 1/2 cups all-purpose flour
   1 cup vanilla baking chips
 1/2 cup quick-cooking oats
 1/2 cup chopped walnuts
 1/4 teaspoon baking powder
 1/4 teaspoon salt

 1/2 cup butter or margarine
   1 cup packed brown sugar
   2 large eggs, lightly beaten
   1 teaspoon vanilla extract

Preheat oven to 350°. Grease and flour an 8- or 9-inch square baking pan.

In a medium bowl, stir flour, chips, oats, nuts, baking powder, and salt; set aside.

In a 3-quart saucepan over medium heat, melt butter. Remove from heat.

Stir in brown sugar until melted. Stir in eggs and vanilla. Add flour mixture and stir until all ingredients are moistened. Spread evenly in baking pan.

Bake 30 minutes or until top is set and golden brown. Cool pan on a wire rack. Cut into squares with a sharp knife.

Cover and store in a cool place.

BLONDE·BROWNIES

Makes 32 (about 2" x 1½") bars

2½ cups all-purpose flour	3 large eggs
½ teaspoon salt	3 teaspoons vanilla extract
1½ cups packed brown sugar	1 package (10 or 12 oz.) peanut butter
¾ cup butter or margarine, softened	chips

Preheat oven to 375°. Coat a 13 x 9 x 2-inch baking pan with non-stick spray.

In a small bowl, stir flour and salt; set aside.

In a large mixer bowl at medium speed, beat brown sugar and butter until fluffy. Beat in eggs and vanilla. At low speed, beat in flour mixture just until moistened. By hand, stir in peanut butter chips. Spread evenly in pan.

Bake 15 to 20 minutes until lightly browned. Cool pan on a wire rack. Cut into bars.

DISAPPEARING·PEANUT·BUTTER·BARS

Makes 32 (about 2" x 1") bars

1   cup chunky peanut butter
½   cup packed brown sugar

1   large egg
1   cup butterscotch chips

Preheat oven to 325°.

In a small bowl, mix peanut butter, brown sugar, and egg until well blended. Press evenly in bottom of an 8- or 9-inch square baking pan.

Bake 20 minutes or until lightly browned. Sprinkle with chips. Cover pan with foil. Bake 5 to 7 minutes longer until chips are softened. Spread chips over peanut butter layer. Cool pan on a wire rack. Cut into bars.

Cover and store in a cool place.

No-Bake · Peanut · Butter · Granola · Bars

Makes 32 (about 2" x 1") bars

$1/2$ cup chunky peanut butter	1 teaspoon vanilla extract
$1/3$ honey	$1\,1/2$ cups granola cereal
$1/2$ cup nonfat dry milk powder	

Lightly butter an 8- or 9-inch square baking pan.

In a medium microwavable bowl, stir peanut butter and honey.

Microwave, uncovered, at 100% power (700 watts) 1 minute. Remove from microwave oven.

Stir in dry milk powder and vanilla until well blended. Stir in granola until well coated with peanut butter mixture. Spoon into pan and press mixture firmly into an even layer.

Let stand 45 minutes or until firm enough to cut. Cut into bars.

Cover tightly to keep bars chewy.